AGAINST FINALITY

CAMBRIDGE UNIVERSITY PRESS
Cambridge, New York, Melbourne, Madrid, Cape Town, Singapore, São Paulo

Cambridge University Press
The Edinburgh Building, Cambridge CB2 8RU, UK

Published in the United States of America by Cambridge University Press, New York

www.cambridge.org
Information on this title: www.cambridge.org/9780521459549

First published 1993

A catalogue record for this publication is available from the British Library

ISBN 978-0-521-45954-9 paperback

Transferred to digital printing 2007

Vice-chancellor, Ladies and Gentlemen,
Inauguration takes its name from the ancient Roman custom of judging the omens for a particular enterprise by studying the flight of birds; and it is customary for an inaugural lecture to provide a similar occasion when the omens for one's subject can be considered, drawing on any auguries that offer themselves.

The nearest thing to an augury that I have noticed recently came last summer in a remark by a prominent and successful literary theorist, who commented that one of the only drawbacks he had discovered to certain kinds of literary theorizing was that if one carried on with them for too long literary texts could lose their power to surprise. The general point he was making must have struck workers in many disciplines. We work towards the goal of some achievement which we hope will hold the field for ever, and yet some other element in our minds advises us to leave room for the unexpected. And indeed the ancient Romans may not have been all that far from a similar recognition, since I suppose that birds never impress us quite so much as when they surprise us: we are walking along a quiet hedgerow when a pheasant suddenly breaks cover with a great commotion; or we are walking along the busy Trumpington Road at night and look down into Hobson's Brook to see a large heron standing quietly in the water.

The last example is of that best sort of surprise which opens out a new dimension in what we thought we thoroughly knew. Some years ago a colleague of mine was looked after in his college rooms by a member of staff who was constantly amazing him by the depths of his conservatism. However innocuous an innovation might seem to be, whether in the nation, the city, the university, or, worst of all, his own college, it would bring out expressions of antagonism and reproach. After this had gone on for a year or two there came the day of a General Election and at last my friend knew exactly what to say. 'Well', he said, 'I suppose you'll be off to vote for the Tories today'. To which he received the straight faced and barely-twinkling reply, 'Oh no, Sir; I hope I know my station'.

Unexpected utterances can occur at every level of human discourse. An obvious example in recent times came from Sir Geoffrey Howe, in his resignation speech to the House of Commons. This was a man whose reputation had steadily grown for remaining loyal to his leader through thick and thin. When he finally felt the time had come to leave he could be expected to say a few dignified words of farewell without breaching that loyalty. Yet the speech, when made, turned out to be dedicated to a different level of loyalty, concluding not in a graceful acceptance of closure but in an equally courteous invitation to insurrection:

> The time has come for others to consider their response to the tragic conflict of loyalty with which I have myself wrestled for perhaps too long.[1]

A commentator wrote shortly afterwards that there could never have been a speech of such effect which had contained in its last sentence the word 'perhaps'. It was a shrewd remark – all the more so when one thinks of the kind of speech that was being undermined. One needs only articulate one or two possibilities: 'There is, perhaps, no alternative'; 'There is, perhaps, no such thing as society' – to see the extraordinary subversive power that can be generated by that lightest of words: once introduce it and the discourse of finality, bearing down on its opponents, is transformed into an invitation to debate and to the mutual exploration of possibilities.

There is of course a part of us that is impatient with the word. When Coleridge was at the height of his enthusiasm for the scheme of Pantisocracy he wrote an agitated reply to his partner Robert Southey, who said he had not received one of his letters:

> They should have arrived on Sunday morning. Perhaps you have not heard from Bath – perhaps – damn perhapses – My God! my God! what a deal of pain you must have suffered . . . [2]

Yet despite his damning, within a year or two Coleridge was writing poetic speculations which revolved round the formula 'And what if?'[3] Over a hundred years later Ezra Pound took up the cause. T. S. Eliot had invited him to work over the typescript of *The Waste Land* and make suggestions. He came to the lines about Mr Eugenides, the Smyrna merchant

> Who asked me, in demotic French,
> To luncheon at the Cannon Street Hotel,
> And perhaps a weekend at the Metropole.

Pound wrote a growling note in the margin: **'Dam Per'apsez'**.[4] Eliot obliged, and the offending word disappeared from *The Waste Land* for ever. But if you have a mind like Eliot's it is not all that easy to damn perhapses permanently. And sure enough, a few years later we find him beginning his *Four Quartets* with the lines

> Time present and time past
> Are both perhaps present in time future,
> And time future contained in time past.

Near the end of the last Quartet, again,

> There is only the fight to recover what has been lost
> And found and lost again and again: and now, under
>   conditions
> That seem unpropitious. But perhaps neither gain nor
>   loss.
> For us there is only the trying . . .

That unhurried altercation between Pound and Eliot reflects an implicit argument that can be traced throughout the nineteenth century between a dominant party inspired by Carlyle, demanding statements of finality that would lead to decisive action, and a few more ruminative writers, such as Tennyson in *In Memoriam*, who combined their acceptance of brute fact with the keeping of a mind open to every possibility.

One of the most versatile strategies for dealing with this situation was devised by Browning, who often chose to write in another's voice. In his poem *Bishop Blougram's Apology* the Bishop, who is widely known for his scepticism, is visited by a journalist who thinks that he has found an easy target for his next article. But Blougram proves to be cleverer than he is expecting, pointing out to him among other things that total scepticism can be as difficult to achieve as total faith:

> Just when we are safest there's a sunset touch,
> A fancy from a flower-bell, some one's death,
> A Chorus-ending from Euripides, –

And that's enough for fifty hopes and fears
As old and new at once as nature's self,
To rap and knock and enter in our soul,
Take hands and dance there, a fantastic ring,
Round the ancient idol, on his base again –
The grand Perhaps![5]

The main effects produced here are worth noticing. The hints and guesses that the Bishop mentions are listed casually, the behaviour of the hopes and fears is presented as grotesque, and the 'grand Perhaps' itself is offered not as the faith that the Bishop himself is supposed to believe in but as an idol. The discussion is taking place, we discover, through at least two layers of irony: and the result is to produce a teasing speculation which is fascinating yet essentially weightless.

The issue that surfaces briefly here bears on a question that I have found being raised in some of my own work. The central task of an English Faculty is usually seen as that of studying the relationship between language and literature on the one hand and something we call 'life' on the other – whether it is the life of the individual or that of the culture. The kind of investigation to which I have devoted myself from time to time stands slightly at an angle to this; I may best describe it briefly as springing from an interest in the effects to be traced in literature and language when the metaphysical authority in the culture gives way to the deferred authority of empirical enquiry. Despite the centrality of this process during the past few centuries we have hardly begun to come to terms with its effects – two of which I want to dwell on in particular. One is that the weighing of words becomes a much more complex matter than it was before, the other that the role of the imagination is thrown increasingly into question.

Such effects were already coming into play in the seventeenth century. Bacon, writing at the beginning of the scientific revolution, asserted that the end of reading was above all things to 'weigh and Consider';[6] and Thomas Sprat thought it to be one of the advantages of instituting the Royal Society that it made possible a more disinterested judging: for even supposing that a man could be found with sufficient grasp to take in the whole of contemporary knowledge, '... how can we be assur'd, that he will hold the scale even?'[7]

Traditionally, the central place for the weighing of words has been in the law. In 1625 Sir Ranulphe Crew, Lord Chief Justice of England, was asked to give judgment in a case concerning the Earldom of Oxford which involved the possible suppression of the noble name of de Vere. In an eloquent speech he described how difficult it was to face such a possibility, yet maintained that, however undesirable, it would not be without precedent:

> I have laboured to make a covenant with myself, that affection may not press upon judgment; for I suppose there is no man, that hath any apprehension of gentry or nobleness, but his affection stands to the continuance of so noble a name and house, and would take hold of a twig or twine-thread to uphold it; and yet time hath his revolution, there must be a period and an end of all temporal things, *finis rerum*, an end of names and dignities, and whatsoever is terrene; and why not of DE VERE?
>
> For where is BOHUN? where's MOWBRAY? where's MORTIMER? &c. nay, which is more, where is PLANTAGANET? They are intombed in the urns and sepulchres of mortality.[8]

The reasoning is that of a man confident that he contains within himself his own centre of gravity, which corresponds in turn to that of the state itself. So sure is he of this that he can actually think of making a covenant *with himself*; like many in the seventeenth century he recognizes in that self a division, yet he is still sufficiently of the old order to feel sure that it is ultimately unified. There is a sense in which the very need to make a covenant at all betrays an awareness that fissures are opening in society, yet they are recognized only in terms of a weighing between judgment and affection. The ordinary world of twigs and twine-thread remains at one with that larger, Latinate universe where time has his revolution.

An alternative answer to the Judge's closing question might, of course, have been, even then, that those whom he names live on in the imagination of Shakespeare; but his own imagining, that of a judge who must concern himself with finality, was closed to such possibilities.

A good deal more weighing went on at that time but I want to move now to the man in the following century who weighed his words more than any other – and who might also be thought of as our greatest protagonist of finality. Samuel Johnson concerned himself, indeed, with the weight of words to an almost obsessive degree. When he was saying farewell to Boswell at Harwich shortly after they first met, and Boswell said that he hoped Johnson would not have to stay long in Harwich, because that would be terrible, Johnson immediately advised him against using big words for little matters – a practice which he held to be very common in France.[9]

It was the same desire to weigh words properly that kept Johnson going during the long years of heroic labour that were devoted to the *Dictionary of the English Language*. In his Preface to the work, he relates how for a time he entertained the gratifying thought that it might be possible by such an enterprise to settle the matter of English words and their meanings finally and for ever, yet he had to accept that this could not be so: even with the most authoritative dictionary in place people would invent new words, or begin to use old ones in new ways; it was a fact of nature and must therefore be honoured.

This recognition of an appeal to nature acted continually to curb Johnson's efforts at finality; and he was further rescued for humanity by the fact that the things he was most final about turned out to be things which were in themselves the very opposite of final. 'Sir, we *know* our will is free – and *there's* an end on't.'[10]

A close reading of Boswell suggests that one of the driving forces behind Johnson's obsessive interest in defining and trying to make final was his desire to construct an edifice of firm significance over an abyss of anxiety. Although Johnson respected the human imagination, he also feared it and in his devotions prayed to be delivered from its corruptions.[11] In *The Rambler* he pictured human beings as 'suspended over the abyss of eternal perdition only by the thread of life, which must soon part by its own weakness, and which the wing of every minute may divide'.[12] Such nightmare fears of endless falling led him to seek the reassurance of those things in nature that offered security. Hence, one might suggest, his continual craving to weigh words properly and also his concern at any phenomenon that compromised the process. He abhorred transgressive wordplay; indeed when he came to define the pun in his *Dictionary* he was hard put to it to find a source for the word which would adequately express his contempt. And it may well be that his distaste was strengthened by his pleasure in certain semantic convergences that are, by contrast, so ingrained in the language, seem to have such a weight of authority behind them, that they not only escape appearing transgressive but can reinforce each other's meanings in ways that seem entirely lawful.

I can best suggest the implications of all this for Johnson by recalling an incident towards the end of his life that tends to stick in the minds of Boswell's readers, for reasons that will shortly become evident.

It came on a day in 1781 when the company and the conversation had been quite exceptionally good: so much so that Boswell found himself whispering to the person next to him at one point, 'I believe this is as much as can be made of life'. Later that evening, Johnson began talking about a friend of his who married a woman who had worked as a printer's devil. There were various pleasantries about this; and then Boswell records that Johnson suddenly said, looking 'very serious and very earnest', 'and she did not disgrace him; the woman had a bottom of good sense'. Boswell continues:

> The word *bottom* thus introduced, was so ludicrous when contrasted with his gravity, that most of us could not forbear tittering and laughing; though I recollect that the Bishop of Killaloe kept his countenance with perfect steadiness, while Miss Hannah More slyly hid her face

behind a lady's back who sat on the same settee with her. His pride could not bear that any expression of his should excite ridicule, when he did not intend it; he therefore resolved to assume and exercise despotick power, glanced sternly around, and called out in a strong tone, 'Where's the merriment?' Then, collecting himself, and looking awful, to make us feel how he could impose restraint, and as it were searching his mind for a still more ludicrous word, he slowly pronounced, 'I say the *woman* was *fundamentally* sensible'; as if he had said, hear this now, and laugh if you dare. We all sat composed as at a funeral.[13]

Boswell ushers us through this story with great skill, so that it becomes simply an anecdote about the loveable Grand Old Man of English letters, the Great Bear, who could be forgiven for throwing his weight about in company because, after all, he was the greatest literary man of his time, and was bound to be disturbed when he found the company amused by an alternative sense which he had not even deigned to record in his dictionary. And we still find it easy to lay aside any anti-authoritarian or other scruples we might have and join in the fun. But there is, I believe, slightly more depth to this anecdote than Boswell quite allows us to see, which emerges more distinctly when we recall some things I was saying just now.

I would draw attention in particular to the word 'gravity'. Gravity is of course a prime example of a word which includes in itself a barely-noticed semantic convergence of the kind I was talking about. We simply do not notice how effortlessly we relate the sense of gravity in nature to that of gravity in human behaviour. And in Johnson's time that convergence was all the more powerful because of the manner in which scientific thinking was dominated by Newton. The power of the word for a thinker such as Johnson owed much to the fact that while Newton's demonstrations had permanently disturbed the metaphysical security of the old universe, they had also offered a sublime replacement: for the new universe being offered was one in which while everything fell nothing fell for ever. All fallings were eventually caught up in that cyclical round of the planets which in turn allows us to enjoy the changes it creates: day and night, the turning of the seasons. Johnson admired Newton deeply, and thought that if he had not been a great scientist he might have been a great epic poet.[14] In his own case, I suspect, the sense of convergence was particularly welcome. He was fond of using his *Dictionary* for didactic purposes; and when he came to define the word 'gravity' he gave pride of place to an example from John Quincy:

> That quality by which all heavy bodies tend towards the centre of the earth, accelerating their motion the nearer they approach towards it, true philosophy has shewn to be unsolveable by any hypothesis and resolved it into the immediate will of the Creator.[15]

One can see how a statement like this might have impressed itself on eighteenth-century moralists, since if gravitation is to be resolved into the immediate will of the Creator it would be natural for them to ask whether it does not display something of the nature of that will in moral terms also. Everyone falls, they might say, yet there is an order of mercy beyond that continues to exist beyond all falling.

If Newton's universe helped to allay the metaphysical anxieties it set up it did so at a distant and impersonal level, however, and the same would be true of any moral analogue that might be adduced. Just as it would be stupid for someone who was in danger of falling from a precipice to start thinking about the larger processes of Newton's universe so in the view of a thinker such as Johnson fallible human beings are fools if they think they can rely directly on the divine mercy.[16] Instead they do well to make their own accommodations with the universe, natural as well as moral; among other things they need, in the language of contemporary moral thought, to 'bottom themselves in principles'.[17] If he reasoned so, it follows that Johnson was not only paying his friend's wife one of the greatest compliments in his power, but one that reached into the whole structure of his thinking, which sought rather desperately at times for evidences of convergence between the natural and the moral. It was evidently deeply disturbing to him to find even so important a word suddenly taking wing as a ludicrous anatomical image and reducing an eighteenth-century company to laughter; when he resolved that action was called for the authority he was trying to impose was not simply his own.

Clergymen were not always able to take the matter of gravity so seriously. In Sterne's *Tristram Shandy* Yorick, who was of a 'mercurial and sublimated . . . composition' and carried 'not one ounce of ballast', 'had an invincible dislike to gravity; – not to gravity as such; – for where gravity was wanted, he would be the most grave or serious of mortal men for days and weeks together; but he was an enemy to the affectation of it, and declared open war against it, only as it appeared a cloak for ignorance, or for folly';[18] as Mark Loveridge has pointed out, moreover, many of the physical misfortunes in the novel, including the central ones, result from random operations of its power.[19] When he ended one of his volumes by commenting on the way in which men of wit and genius have confounded the straight line with the 'line of GRAVITATION',[20] he may have been offering a hint as to the orbiting nature of his own narrative. Lewis Carroll, who had evidently reflected a good deal on the ways in which semantic convergences that normally form part of the natural dispositions of the language can surprise by passing into a looking glass world and exploiting themselves transgressively, twined the threads between Johnson and Sterne more tightly together: his Snark, you will recall, 'always looks grave at a pun'.

And Johnson himself was not normally so heavy-handed in company; although he liked to have the last word, he also enjoyed the natural run of conversation. On one occasion his garrulous old college friend Edwards, meeting him after nearly half a century, said in the course of conversation, 'You are a philosopher, Dr Johnson. I have tried too in my time to be a philosopher; but I don't know how, cheerfulness was always breaking in'. Johnson showed no particular displeasure; and when Boswell implied that Edwards's garrulity was the mark of a weak man he accepted that this was a man who had passed through life without experience but claimed to prefer the company of such people over that of those who did not talk readily, since at least they kept the conversation going.[21] The currency of company was a welcome antidote to the transfixing anxieties that could beset him in private.

Some of his younger contemporaries gave a greater rein to cheerfulness. As a young man William Blake was impatient with Johnson, whom he pictured in flight as a 'Bat with Leathern wing, / Winking & blinking';[22] he had little time for any weighing of words, let alone an obsessive one. Unlike Johnson, again, he thought it still possible to produce a poetry that would have metaphysical validity, his own favoured method being to let his imagination and his words fly free – or, on occasion, to compact them into riddles. In the process he often paid the price of forfeiting communication with his audience, but he was content to do so in the interests of showing the world what it might be like to think in a manner that was fully independent.

Others who shared his enthusiasm for writing metaphysically were more interested in communication. Coleridge, too, believed in the possibility of a poetry that soared intellectually, but he was also anxious to be heard by his contemporary audience. He was to find, nevertheless, that the fissure which kept opening between Johnson's anxieties and eighteenth-century empiricism could not be bridged as easily as one might hope. In one of his early poems (the punningly titled *Religious Musings*) an attempt of his to write a poetry of metaphysical sublimity includes the lines,

> There is one Mind, one omnipresent Mind,
> Omnific. His most holy name is LOVE.
> Truth of subliming import![23]

I once heard a critic remark that when he came to the word 'omnific', followed by the words 'truth of subliming import', he found himself irresistibly conjuring up the image of an eighteenth-century bishop, holding forth on truths of subliming import from a seated plump body and flowing surplice which were miming the contours of his words even as he spoke. That was a little unfair to Coleridge, who aimed to use the word 'subliming' more actively, but it demonstrates the extent to which aspiring energies can be held down by the residual weight of the words they are trying to lift.

Coleridge, meanwhile, was increasingly aware of a nature in which firm metaphysical bearings were ceasing to exist, and was to describe such a world brilliantly in *The Ancient Mariner*; as he did so the possibility of writing a positive metaphysical poetry moved further and further away. His visit to Germany impressed him with the fact that metaphysics itself was now the subject of the critical philosophy, so that the successful metaphysician was likely to be not a poet but an analytical thinker. When he tried to divine his future as a poet by looking to the flight of his mind he found that the auguries were not good, writing gloomily of trains of thought which,

> when I wished to write a poem beat up Game of far other kind – instead of a Covey of poetic Partridges with whirring wings of music, or wild Ducks *shaping* their rapid flight in forms always regular (a still better image of verse) up came a metaphysical Bustard, urging it's slow, heavy, laborious, earth-skimming flight, over dreary and level Wastes.[24]

He was coming to see that the genius of the nineteenth century, so far as it had one, would be the genius of criticism. Later he was to say that Horne Tooke, author of *The Diversions of Purley*, should not have called his book 'Winged Words' but 'Living Words'[25] – a preference which is implicit in his own developing work on philology. He never stopped being a poet, and he admired particularly the poem by Giordano Bruno which proclaimed the possibility of making metaphysics take wing,[26] but he restrained himself from further attempts at such a metaphysical soaring of his own (except by way of love-poetry), looking rather at the ways in which words might be regarded as living organisms. (One of the many results of that intricate process was of course his introduction of the term 'practical criticism', which made him a distant founding figure for a distinctive and central feature of Cambridge English.)

Some of the next generation were in their turn impatient at what they saw as an over-preoccupation with intellectual niceties. Shelley admired Coleridge yet also believed it might be possible for a visionary metaphysics to take in everything that was being discovered in contemporary science and still preserve its coherence. Accordingly, he continued to pursue the flight of the mind in an adventurous and unpondering fashion, finding his best augury in the skylark that could sing and soar until it disappeared from sight. In the process, however, he discovered that the social weights which his hero Rousseau had identified as oppressing human beings in modern society could weigh more heavily on his consciousness than he had anticipated. His poem to the West Wind included the lines

> A heavy weight of hours has bowed
> One too like thee, restless and free and proud.

This incompatibility between his devotion to a flight of the mind that he hoped would be for the benefit of mankind and the weight of responsibility involved in being human was to be projected on to Rousseau himself when he was introduced into his late and perplexed poem *The Triumph of Life*:

> . . . like one who with the weight
> Of his own words is staggered, wearily
> He paused'.[27]

Shelley's poetry was read enthusiastically by writers of the new generation such as Tennyson and Browning, and his political ideas were an inspiration to radicals of the next age, but as the records of the ways in which he had shrugged his own human responsibilities came to the knowledge of the Victorian reading public his literary reputation drooped. It was not until the cause of liberalism took a new lease of life at the turn of the century that writers began to turn back and re-evaluate his achievement. Virginia Woolf, for whom Shelley was always to be an important presence, wrote in her youth of the aspiration in her art as being to

> achieve a symmetry by means of infinite discords, showing all the tracts of the mind's passage through the world; achieve in the end, some kind of whole made of shivering fragments; to me this seems the natural process; the flight of the mind.[28]

In the last summer of her life, likewise, she wrote

> and I read my Shelley at night. How delicate & pure & musical and uncorrupt he & Coleridge read, after the left wing group. How lightly and firmly they put down their feet, and how they sing; & how they compact; & fuse; and deepen. I wish I cd invent a new critical method – something swifter & lighter & more colloquial & yet intense:

> more to the point & less composed; more fluid & following the flight, than my Common Reader essays. The old problem: how to keep the flight of the mind, yet be exact.[29]

While Shelley and Virginia Woolf were being faithful to the flight of the mind another strain of writing in the nineteenth century picked up and made central what had been for Virginia Woolf no more than a counterweight. This enterprise, which aimed to achieve exactness before contemplating any flight, was essentially one of assaying. The writers involved – again a select group – placed their primary reliance upon an honouring of the weight of words. Gerard Manley Hopkins, for example, writes in one of his lectures on rhetoric,

> We may think of words as heavy bodies, as indoor or out of door objects of nature or of man's art. Now every visible or palpable body has a centre of gravity round which it is in balance and a centre of illumination or highspot or quickspot up to which it is lighted or down to which it is shaded. The centre of gravity is like the accent of stress, the highspot like the accent of pitch.[30]

It is a paragraph well worth pondering for its evidence of what Hopkins was doing in his own poetry. When he looked to nature for an embodiment of his own poetic ideal the augury he found was not, as with Shelley, that of a skylark soaring and singing out of sight but of a kestrel, which because of its skill in riding blustery winds had also come to be known as a 'windhover'.[31] In his poem about it, which he thought the best he ever wrote, he describes his delight in watching the bird balance and rebalance in the air until the very mastery of what it is doing generates the sense of a further poise – between the material qualities of brute beauty and valour and act and the more elusive graces of air, pride and plume.[32] Whenever that poise so manifests itself it is also an illumination, Hopkins's 'highspot or quickspot', releasing something like a flash of creative fire. It becomes the fitting emblem for a poetry that calls on the reader to balance and weigh before it will release its meaning.

There are other writers in whom we recognize something of the same preoccupation. John Crowe Ransom wrote that 'the density or connotativeness of poetic language reflects the world's density',[33] while William Empson commented on one occasion that a word may become a 'kind of solid entity, able to direct opinion'.[34] For a more extreme exposition we turn to Ezra Pound, whose father had been an assayer, literally so, at the Philadelphia mint. His son was to recall the impression made on him as a boy during a currency crisis when he watched half naked men with open gas flares shovelling four million tarnished coins into the counting machines.[35] One senses in Pound himself a corresponding and incessant need to try the currency – indeed he often found it hard to separate in his mind the currency of language from the monetary currency of the society in which it circulated: in both cases he wanted to restore it to a state where it need not rely on credit. We all know to what sad ends his obsessive urge for finality eventually led him; yet his enterprise is still one that can be honoured as we honour Virginia Woolf's: it brings out with clarity what can be achieved in positive terms by someone who concentrates wholly on the need to try for exactness – whether of the word, the phrase, or, above all, the image.

Shelley and Woolf and Hopkins and Pound each display in different ways the intensity that is generated by a need to bridge the gap between precise weighing and valid imagining. They stand somewhat to the side of that main body of literature which concerns itself with the more immediate fate of human beings in the culture, harking back rather to the problems created as scientific language achieved its overwhelming authority; yet their having each gained a distinctive place of their own in the canon suggests that such problems are not perceived as entirely irrelevant to that fate.

The weighing of words need not always be a matter of such intensity. We might for example look at Jane Austen. At the beginning of *Persuasion* she alludes lightly to the process in introducing her heroine, whose father, Sir Walter Elliot, is much preoccupied by names and dignities and whatsoever is terrene – so much so that he judges his family entirely by such standards, his favourite being the one daughter who has kept her looks. Anne Elliot, by contrast,

> with an elegance of mind and sweetness of character, which must have placed her high with any people of real understanding, was nobody with either father or sister: her word had no weight; her convenience was always to give way; – she was only Anne.[36]

In one sense the whole plot of the novel (one of her more questioning narratives) can be seen to evolve from that pause to weigh incompatibles.

Or again, we might look at James Carker, the manager of the House of Dombey in Dickens's novel. More than a decade before the publication of *The Origin of Species* we find Dickens dwelling constantly on his prominent set of teeth. ('A cat, or a monkey, or a hyena, or a death's head could not have shown . . . more teeth at one time . . . ')[37] On a crucial occasion Mr Carker opens a letter:

> It was in the writing of his great chief, Mr Dombey, and dated from Leamington. Though he was a quick reader of all other letters Mr Carker read this slowly: weighing the words as he went, and bringing every tooth in his head to bear on them.[38]

What is given here directly and uncomplicatedly is the assaying enterprise in its lowest form. Mr Carker weighs every word for its potential of profit or loss; the trying of every word with his teeth suggests that he even sees the words as coins which can be tested for their genuineness. And of course the teeth also suggest something more sinister – an instinct to consume which eventually recoils upon him in a literal devouring by one of the new monsters of industrialism. Unlike Ezra Pound, who refers the health of the currency to that of the people who produce it, Mr Carker's dealings with words express the rapacity of a weighing for one purpose only.

People with a more practical role in Victorian culture often felt an obligation to weigh their words. Mr Gladstone prided himself on doing so.[39] Or we might listen to T. H. Huxley, speaking to the Working Men's Club and Institute in 1877 on the need for Technical Education. Although he was somewhat conservative in his views about how far people should be educated, Huxley was strong on the need to provide opportunities for everyone who could benefit. And when it came to scientific genius, he had no hesitation at all:

I weigh my words, when I say that if the nation could purchase a potential Watt, or Davy, or Faraday, at the cost of a hundred thousand pounds down, he would be dirt-cheap at the money.[40]

In one sense we recognize a familiar language here: it belongs to the kinds of statement that university professors and administrators constantly feel they must make when trying to persuade a reluctant government to disburse further resources for teaching and research. Huxley goes on to assert (as they do) that scientists, who may seem to spend a great deal of time making no solid contribution to the economy at all can also make discoveries which will more than make up for that in straightforward commercial terms. Yet while it is hard to let so persuasive an argument go by default, those who know what a university is really about must always have a distant sense of potential betrayal when they find themselves speaking in this mode, an awareness of how easily such arguments can be used in turn to back a funding of universities purely on grounds of demonstrable commercial benefit.

Huxley himself would no doubt have resisted such a construction on what he was saying. And in fact the very way that he presents his case helps first to undermine and then to open out his own argument. By the very stress he places on the weighing of words he helps to conjure up the image of a giant pair of scales, with a Davy or a Faraday on the one side and a hundred thousand gold sovereigns, cash down, on the other. Once made literal the image becomes ludicrous, bringing home the absurdity of trying to weigh creativity. Scientific discoveries, also, call for an exercise of the imagination;

and not every distinguished scientist exhibits his or her full potentialities in childhood. One of Cambridge's most distinguished scientists was informed by a schoolmaster that he was the worst scientist his school had ever turned out.

Although there have been many imaginative scientific discoveries since Davy and Faraday the fault line between the processes of weighing and imagining that I have been trying to indicate still shows itself from time to time in the culture. In January 1993 Steven Weinberg published his book *Dreams of a Final Theory*, in which he argued the case for persuading the United States government to release the eight billion dollars which are still needed to carry through the Superconducting Super Collider project, a fifty-three-mile tunnel under Texas in which it will be possible to generate energy on such a scale as to facilitate an unprecedented series of experiments, taking us further towards those culminating ones which, he believes, will provide us once and for all with a final theory of the universe. Professor Weinberg is quick to point out that the establishment of such a final theory will not mean an end to science, since there will still be an immense amount to do in chemistry and biology. He even observes at one point that the results of experiments are sometimes surprising, and that when such results have embodied the discovery of some new phenomenon such as x-rays, or the particles which are known as 'strange', they are the experiences that have, in his own words, brought most joy to the hearts of experimentalists.[41] Yet he believes that the converging logic of twentieth-century scientific theory will enable those who conduct the ultimate experiments to make a final statement about the universe; and if their results turn out to follow that logic (as he believes they must) the final universe that emerges will be one that is – to quote his own terms again – 'chilly' and 'impersonal' and, also, very 'beautiful'.[42]

When Weinberg looks for an augury for humanity he finds it once again in a bird – in his case the sparrow which long ago flew in and out of a banqueting hall and provided Bede's history with a memorable emblem for human life.[43] He finds that image of human life as a feasting and a flight very attractive, and has in fact only one *caveat* to enter. Honour, he says, demands that we resist the temptation of believing that there is anything outside the banqueting hall. The so-called common-sense logic which says that if a sparrow flies into a hall it must have come from somewhere is to be countered by a logic that converges overwhelmingly on the conclusion that there is nothing outside. If that is so, any sense of the bird's coming can be no more than a pleasing illusion.

One might expect such a book to make depressing reading. The fact that it does not owes much to two things: the exhilarating anthropocentrism of its thinking, as it provides more and more reasons for supposing that human beings are so stationed as to be able to understand the universe, and the clarity and verve of the writing, producing a humane matrix to receive the series of creative impulses it records. In doing so it reminds us that there is such a thing as the Muse of Science, and that the Muses, at least, do not seem to be interested in any conception of finality.

A similar fault line between weighing and imagining is to be traced also in the world of modern literature. Late twentieth-century fiction has been quite extraordinarily fertile and inventive; indeed one hardly notices that there is a problem at all until one turns to the institution of literary prizes, which directs that novels must all in some sense be weighed one against another. The reported deliberations of the judges demonstrate how, faced with a mountain of reading, they tend to move inexorably in one of two directions. Either they are drawn to look for the most imaginative achievement, which is brave but involves the almost impossible task of weighing one person's imagination against another's, or they look increasingly for some element of demonstrable weight in the novel itself. The latter search may cause them to find attractions in a novel with a strong basis in verifiable fact – the mode of writing that has given rise to the term 'faction'.

The existence of this problem is evident to some of the novelists themselves, who have found enterprising ways of dealing with it. Milan Kundera's novel *The Unbearable Lightness of Being*, for example, is constructed around a presentation of human experience in modern societies – free or otherwise – against a questioning of Parmenides' statement that weight is always negative and lightness always positive. It is an ingenious way of bringing together the novelist's weighing and imagining while at another level contriving to keep them in separate compartments.

In much the same way the ultimate problems of science and those of fiction can sometimes be seen interpenetrating one another, as in the recent attempts by Daniel Dennett to solve the problem of consciousness by seeing the so-called self as a capacity for generating stories about one's experience and so proposing as his definition of self the phrase a 'centre of narrative gravity'[44] – a phrase which Virginia Woolf might have enjoyed thinking about.

There are various directions in which one could continue from here, and there are certainly issues here that I myself want to go on exploring. But my business on this occasion being primarily with auguries I want now to suggest that the issues which sometimes emerge into clarity in writers such as Hopkins or Woolf, and which remain intricately interwoven in twentieth-century thinking and writing, have also appeared very strikingly in the past when poets have been thinking defensively – that they have sometimes displayed what is at stake in the processes of weighing and imagining most clearly when responding to their own experiences of loss.

It is in tune with this perception that some recent writers have found it profitable to enter into a more intricate engagement with the past. Not only are such writers licensed to explore history imaginatively as well as factually but they can draw on the past of literature itself, so that a novel may become in itself a form of creative criticism. In A. S. Byatt's novella 'Conjugial Love' – which among other things performs this service for Tennyson's *In Memoriam* – a character comments at one point on the peculiar force of a stanza addressed to the boat that is bringing back Arthur Hallam's body from Vienna to England:[45]

> Thou bringst the sailor to his wife.
> And travelled men from foreign lands
> And letters unto trembling hands;
> And, thy dark freight, a vanished life.[46]

The effect to which attention is drawn is the complex one induced by writing of a vanished life as a freight, by weighing an absence; it is an insight that develops further as one notices how the ambiguities are already prepared for in the preceding line by the word 'trembling'. The uncertainty opened up by that word (news of great joy or great loss?) is extended in the last line, which not only weighs the meaningless heaviness of the filled coffin against the endless lightness of the vanishing but then revolves 'lightness' into a different dimension as the reader recalls how elsewhere that vanished life is presented as an illumination. Yet reborne consciousness of the vanishing turns all back into an oppressive weight. As these knowledges, meaningless or elusively significant, move one against the other an eddy is set up in the line before the narrative can be resumed. That eddy, a working of words between weight and lightness, light and dark, could, if the reader so wished, be endless; it can also reach out to envelop and interpret the whole poem. Oppression is weighed against imponderables in lasting paradox.

The poet who best exhibits the possibilities of these effects is Wordsworth, who is, with Milton and Tennyson, one of our great defensive poets, those who are most concerned with loss. Generally he is on the side of those whom I have referred to as the assayers, finding one of his most natural voices in phrases such as 'I must believe, do all I can ... ' or 'For this loss I would believe abundant recompense'. Some of his most powerful images also are those of weight. In *The Prelude* he describes how in his boyhood the idea of London had always lived in his imagination with an aura of romance; yet when he

finally entered the city and saw nothing but vulgarity
and meanness in every direction,

> A weight of ages did at once descend
> Upon my heart . . .

Yet it is also characteristic of Wordsworth that this
weighing has no finality, since his mind simultaneously
finds itself caught up by another process:

> – no thought embodied, no
> Distinct remembrances, but weight and power,
> Power growing with the weight . . . [47]

That unexpected turn, by which he has no sooner
become oppressed by weight than he becomes conscious
of a growing power, is highly Wordsworthian. Another
example can be found in the lines with which he ends
his famous account of the young boy who learned how
to mimic the hootings of owls so successfully that they
would hoot back, until in an eerie moment of silence the
actual scene in nature around him would impress itself
conclusively on his mind and memory. The description
concludes with an evocation of

> that uncertain heaven, received
> Into the bosom of the steady lake.[48]

When Coleridge first read these lines he wrote that if
he had found them running wild in the deserts of Arabia
he would immediately have shrieked out 'Wordsworth!'[49]
And there is indeed something peculiarly characteristic in
the way those last two lines bring together incompatibles
and seem to hold them in a unity without actually doing
so. If one tries to see the scene in one's mind, its unity

eludes capture. One can visualize the moving clouds that are being reflected in the water, and one can visualize the steady lake, but one cannot hold them finally together – one will always see either the reflected movement or the still form of the lake, playing one against the other. The elements of the scene remain compacted together, in other words, but cannot be fixed into a single image.

Because Wordsworth presented himself as a man who wanted to write simply, it can still be difficult to see how complex some of his effects are. Sometimes, for example, he can produce an unusual kind of semantic convergence by which a word that has diverse meanings is so deployed as to leave those meanings in a trembling equilibrium of incompatibles. For a simple example of what I mean I would cite the line in which he recalls the emotional effects of the French Revolution: 'the senselessness of joy was then sublime'.[50] The immediate reference is to an echoed ecstasy in which people had forgotten themselves in delight at being presented with a new-found freedom; yet that very word 'senselessness' is immediately shot through with a requiring admonition, recalling the madness of the events that followed, in the Terror. And the existence of that fearful ambiguity throws into relief the importance of the word 'sense' itself, which Empson investigated to such effect in *Complex Words*. It suggests, in another way, the importance of being 'fundamentally sensible'.

Wordsworth's ability to weigh incompatibles emerges with clarity in some lines addressed to Coleridge in *The Prelude* in which he applauds his friend's concentration on the sense of unity:

> Hard task to analyse a soul, in which
> Not only general habits and desires,
> But each most obvious and particular thought –
> Not in a mystical and idle sense,
> But in the words of reason deeply weighed –
> Hath no beginning.[51]

'The words of reason deeply weighed' here turn out to do no more than state a negative. And yet that negative is indeed of importance for Wordsworth, since the lack of a beginning does not necessarily lose everything in a primeval darkness or nothingness: it may simply indicate a perpetual cyclical process. It is one of the reasons that the imagery of streams played such a central role in his poetry.

In one of the best known of Wordsworth's poems, the one that begins 'A slumber did my spirit seal' and which Coleridge described on first reading as a 'sublime Epitaph'[52], his skill at the weighing of words can be seen in action:

Epitaph

> A slumber did my spirit seal,
>   I had no human fears:
> She seem'd a Thing, that could not feel
>   The touch of earthly years.
>
> No motion has she now, no force;
>   She neither hears nor sees,
> Mov'd round in Earth's diurnal course
>   With rocks, & stones, and trees![53]

The two stanzas of the poem set together and weigh incompatible experiences. In the first the human imagination is transported into a state of trance so absolute that not only is the sense of mortality suspended, but even the sense of time. And then, abruptly, we move to the second stanza, which shows how treacherous such an imagining appears when contemplated under the realization of loss. The living statuesque quality of the original scene is now transfixed into a deathliness – that of a body resigned to the elements.

It could be a depressing poem; but once again such an effect is averted. By inviting us to contemplate the total scene, Wordsworth brings out that ultimate mercy of the Newtonian universe mentioned earlier – that in the solar system things end neither in an endless falling nor in a fixed stasis but in a reversion to the cycling processes of ordinary nature. There is also a strange opening out at the very end of the poem. If Wordsworth had wanted to induce a sense of utter desolation he would surely have ended the poem with the deadness of rocks. By ending it as he does he again imports a strange sense of lightening – a marginal consolation, admittedly, but still recognizable as such, since if we have to contemplate so bleak a prospect there is something just a little more consoling in the idea of being rolled round with trees. And in Wordsworth's increasingly rare visionary states, I am sure, trees sometimes seemed to be sealed in a slumber.[54]

A weighing of an even more subtle kind can be found in a poem written, he tells us, a few years after the death of his young daughter, which left him in such desolation that he could not bear to read fiction – not even, for a time, Spenser:[55]

> Surprised by joy – impatient as the Wind
> I turned to share the transport – Oh! with whom

> But Thee, deep buried in the silent tomb,
> That spot which no vicissitude can find?
> Love, faithful love, recalled thee to my mind –
> But how could I forget thee? Through what power,
> Even for the least division of an hour,
> Have I been so beguiled as to be blind
> To my most grievous loss! – That thought's return
> Was the worst pang that sorrow ever bore,
> Save one, one only, when I stood forlorn,
> Knowing my heart's best treasure was no more;
> That neither present time, nor years unborn
> Could to my sight that heavenly face restore.[56]

It is a moving poem, and I would not want anything I say about it to detract from its immediate effect But it is also one of the most complex that Wordsworth ever wrote, and its intricacy, once perceived, reinforces its power to move. Near its beginning there is, as it happens, an inaugurating moment of a literal kind: 'I turned to share the transport – oh with whom . . . ?' Before the opening statement could be completed, Shelley took it up in mid-flight, as it were, to provide the climax for a poem of his own. In 'The Question'[57] the poet has a vision of winter transformed into spring and imagines himself picking a bunch of the visionary flowers that result; he concludes

> I hastened to the spot whence I had come,
> That I might there present it! – Oh! to whom?

Shelley's last line was then picked out by that great master-mistress of elegy and reinauguration Virginia Woolf, who gave it to her character Rhoda in *The Waves*. Rhoda lives at the very edge of things and in consequence repeatedly experiences life as a nightmare falling or drowning, followed by a rebirth. Her regret that she can never share the resulting sense of joy with others is summed up in a phrase which becomes a kind of refrain: 'I will gather my flowers and present them – Oh! to whom?'[58]

In the creative acts of Shelley and Woolf Wordsworth's opening two lines are cut off to become a statement about the difficulty of communication: the experience of flight and check is dwelt on before it can extend itself into the sense of human loss that comes at the turn of the line: 'with whom / But thee . . . ?' Once that loss has been registered in Wordsworth's poem the perspective changes, transposing us into a more shadowy region where we may find ourselves recalling that Hermes, the winged messenger of the gods, is also the guide of the underworld. Inauguration ceases but mercurial resonances are sustained, linking Wordsworth's response with other literary texts in which a writer tries to cope with the same experience. I am thinking, for example, of Philip Larkin's poem 'Reference Back', in which the experience of playing a particular jazz record transports him back to adolescence and a fractile relationship with his mother:

> We are not suited to the long perspectives
> Open at every instant of our lives.
> They link us to our losses.[59]

A further variation on the theme is given by Proust, for whom the unbuttoning of his boots in a moment of weariness unexpectedly summons from the past his relationship with his grandmother in its totality. In the same instant his realization for the first time that she is lost for ever translates him into a state of alternating perceptions:

> I could not understand, and I struggled to endure the anguish of this contradiction: on the one hand an existence, a tenderness, surviving in me as I had known them, that is to say created for me, a love which found in me so totally its complement, its goal, its constant lodestar . . . and on the other hand, as soon as I had relived that bliss as though it were present, feeling it shot through by the certainty, throbbing like a recurrent pain, of an annihilation that had effaced my image of that tenderness, had destroyed that existence, retrospectively abolished our mutual predestination, made of my grandmother, at the moment when I had found her again as in a mirror, a mere stranger . . . [60]

One turns from these inaugurations and resonances to the things in Wordsworth's poem that are distinctively his. The first is the phrase 'impatient as the wind', another example of the process described earlier by which Wordsworth can weigh disparate meanings within a single word or phrase. 'Impatient as the wind' links primarily with the imagery of joy in *The Prelude*, when he describes the delights of youthful freedom, skating, rambling or on horseback;[61] yet the phrase recoils on itself as it recalls another occasion, when he stood in a high and windswept place, waiting impatiently for the delayed horses that were to take him home and not yet knowing that they would take him back to the death of his father and the end of his childhood. The experience as a whole would be remembered as one of the two central among his 'spots of time'. In the present poem, by contrast, the word 'spot', which comes three lines later, simply seems – on first reading, at least – a strangely casual one to use in referring to a grave.

Another word deserves to be paused over: 'vicissitude'. That alertest of critics F. R. Leavis recorded the surprise which he experienced on coming to it in the fourth line –

> . . . a surprise in the sense that one doesn't at first know how to read it, the turn in feeling and thought being so unexpected. For the line, instead of insisting on the renewed overwhelming sense of loss, appears to offset it with a consideration on the other side of the account.[62]

It is a crucial point, but I believe there is more that can be said. Dr Leavis's prime touchstone for the reading of literature was always to be found in Shakespeare. Now 'vicissitude' is not itself a Shakespearean word (or not unless he really *was* Bacon, in which case he wrote a fine concluding essay on the subject[63]). But vicissitude is certainly an ever-present Shakespearean concept, coming straight through from the Middle Ages to haunt his history plays and, more subtly, his tragedies, with unexpected misfortunes. And it is perfectly true that if you read the line in this sense an unexpected relief seems to be offered. If the grave is a spot which no misfortune can touch that is surely something to be thankful for.

At the same time there had been in the recent literature of Wordsworth's time a tendency to look at the word rather differently, referring to the changes of day and night and of the seasons as graces within nature. Cowper, for example, wrote in his poem 'Hope':

> Nature indeed vouchsafes for our delight
> The sweet vicissitudes of day and night . . .

Gray, too, wrote a fragmentary ode 'On the Pleasure arising from Vicissitude'. Once one begins to weigh that sense of the word against the Shakespearean it acquires both a negative and positive charge, with the pleasurable meaning of vicissitude returning again and again to enforce that very sense of loss which Leavis found lacking.

If we now ask what kind of sonnet this is, we discover its form to be Miltonic rather than Shakespearean; yet there is a good deal in the language and movement to remind us rather of Shakespeare's sonnets – words such as 'heart', 'treasure' and 'heavenly'. It is when we get to the end that we see Wordsworth forced to argue against the conclusion to which such elements in the sonnets might be seeming to point. Sonnet 30, 'When to the sessions of sweet silent thought / I summon up remembrance of things past', concludes,

> But if the while I think on thee, dear friend,
> All losses are restored and sorrows end.

The final words of this poem refuse to accept such an ending. If there is a Shakespearean world here it is a more desolate one than the world of the sonnets.

The true grounding author here is rather Milton, whose presence is established in the very opening word. We are all familiar with the experience of offering a child something which we hope will be a welcome surprise and then being startled in our turn when it stomps out of the room in anger or simply dissolves in a flood of tears. The moment of surprise catches human beings, small or large, off balance, unable for a moment to weigh things at all, so that it is not altogether unpredictable that the infravening emotion should be other than the one appealed to. And the moment of unbalance on which this poem is to turn is already prophesied in its opening phrase, where those who are familiar with Milton will immediately pick up an admonition. During the War in Heaven the early successes of the rebel angels filled them with exhilaration and an assurance that they were bound to win; but at the first setback, with the prospect that they might after all lose, they were

> with pale fear surpris'd,
> Then first with fear surpris'd . . . [64]

That alternative, admonitory undertone is then picked up in other strikingly Miltonic words, such as 'transport', 'beguile' and 'forlorn', all of which, in *Paradise Lost*, are associated with angers and desolations. The language of Milton is particularly apposite because what is being described here is an apparent treachery of the imagination.

Yet Milton could not invoke *Paradise Lost* without invoking the whole poem – weighing Milton against himself as it were; and there is a yet further depth to one or two of the words which suggests the nature of that weighing.

The first clue comes in a place where we have noticed it before in Wordsworth. In one sense the concluding line is as final as it could possibly be; yet the very last word has Miltonic resonances of quite another kind. Once again the reader whose mind is attuned to *Paradise Lost* may well pick up a strange echo, its source the beginning of a line at the outset where Milton sets out to tell how sin

> Brought Death into the World, and all our woe,
> With loss of *Eden*, till one greater man
> Restore us, and regain the blissful seat . . . [65]

'Sing heavenly Muse . . . ' he continues; and the opening as a whole conveys a sense of visionary dedication. Wordsworth's own corresponding sense was associated in part with a childhood when, like other visionaries such as Blake and John Henry Newman, he had found it hard to believe that the physical world was the real one. That lingering sense (witnessed to among other things by his regularly placing the Immortality Ode at the end of his collected poems) must always have kept alive in him the sense of a Miltonic 'perhaps'. Perhaps the most bitter desolations, including even the one described here, might yet open out into a quite different ordering of things.

We may read on in *Paradise Lost*. In Book Seven Milton describes how God set lights in the firmament of heaven

> T'illuminate the Earth, and rule the Day
> In thir vicissitude . . . [66]

In the previous book he has already described how the same process is found in Heaven itself:

> There is a Cave
> Within the Mount of God, fast by his Throne,
> Where light and darkness in perpetual round
> Lodge and dislodge by turns, which makes through Heav'n
> Grateful vicissitude, like Day and Night . . . [67]

The true appositeness of 'vicissitude' to Wordsworth's poem derives, I think, not simply from its introducing echoes both of Shakespearean desolation and of an eighteenth-century consolation which weighs with it in such a way as to intensify it, but from its ability, even while it is doing that, and without in any way compromising Wordsworth's sceptical and stoic stance, to leave glimmering on the horizon the distant light of a Miltonic 'perhaps'. Perhaps in some unimaginable reordering of existence the intimations of immortality that haunted Wordsworth's childhood imagination might yet come to be realized; and in that case the grave which now seems to be such a permanent and fixing spot, would turn out to have been no more (and no less) than a 'spot of time'.

We return to the opening word of the poem, and to the experience of unexpected joy that inaugurated it. And here too I suspect a further dimension, again to be opened up by the account of the War in Heaven, which had a significance of its own for Romantic writers. Although Milton's universe had been subverted by Newton's theories, the events of the War could still be read as an allegory of the working of that supreme poetic imagination which made Milton for them the hero of his own poem.

Later in the account the rebel angels unveil their big surprise, an engine which they believe will turn the balance of the battle decisively in their favour. And when it has been let off they taunt the loyal angels with their newly revealed superiority. Belial, gloating to Satan, unleashes a volley of bad puns:

> Leader the terms we sent were terms of *weight*
> Of *hard contents*, and full of *force* urg'd home,
> Such as we might perceive *amus'd* them all,
> And *stumbl'd* many: who receives them right
> Had need from head to foot well *understand* . . . [68]

However, the rebels are to discover that the Muse is not to be dismissed so easily and that they have not fully grasped the semantics of heaven, by which terms of weight can be overcome by arguments of light. Subsequent attacks and counter-attacks lead to the moment when God the Father decides to intervene. There emerges the chariot of paternal deity, the description of its beauties culminating in a close-up view of its charioteer, the Son:

> beside him hung his Bow
> And Quiver with three-bolted Thunder stor'd,
> And from about him fierce Effusion rould
> Of smoke and bickering flame, and sparkles dire . . . [69]

If this is powerful, it is also a little disappointing: it suggests that God is about to win simply by superior technology – and a technology which in any case looks rather antiquated by the superior standards of twentieth-century warfare. But immediately there is an abrupt turn in the verse, as Milton's imagination suddenly takes wing. From contemplating the chariot at close quarters we are transported to view the host that surround it – so endless that attempts at numbering give way to recognition of an overwhelming illumination:

> Attended with ten thousand thousand Saints,
> He onward came, farr off his coming shon . . .

Wordsworth was to praise those lines as being work of the highest form of imagination. Everything else, he said, was lost almost and merged in the splendour of that indefinite abstraction 'His coming!'[70] And one sees what he means: in those words simple light is overcome by illumination, absence transformed into presence.

Wordsworth must also have experienced an especial kindling of pleasure – though essentially private and elusive – as he read on in that passage. Milton goes on to expand his great moment of illumination, making it burst out like a firework in the Latinate 'illustrious':

> Hee on the wings of Cherube rode sublime
> On the Crystallin Skie, on Saphir Thron'd.
> Illustrious farr and wide.[71]

At this point, however, a 'but' shifts his and the reader's view abruptly, as his imagination suddenly stoops, this time to contemplate a less obvious, counterweighing heroism and to remember the angels who had succeeded in standing fast against those who were trying to impose their own version of finality – a finality which would have left no place for the Muses. The passage runs on

> but by his own
> First seen, them unexpected joy surpriz'd . . .

NOTES

(Place of publication is London unless otherwise shown)

1 Report in *The Times*, 14 November 1990.
2 Coleridge, *Collected Letters*, ed. E. L. Griggs, 6 volumes (Oxford 1956–71) vol. I, p. 109.
3 See his *Poetical Works*, ed. E. H. Coleridge, 2 volumes (Oxford 1912) vol. I, 102, 124.
4 T. S. Eliot, *The Waste Land: A Facsimile and Transcription of the Original Drafts including the Annotations of Ezra Pound* (1971) p. 30. Pound made a similar annotation to a later 'perhaps': 'Perhaps be *damned*'. See *ibid.*, 44.
5 'Bishop Blougram's Apology', lines 182–90. *Poetical Works*, ed. Ian Jack (Oxford 1970) p. 650.
6 'Of Studies. L.': Sir Francis Bacon. *The Essayes or Counsels, civill and Morall* [1625], ed. M. Kiernan (Oxford 1985) p. 153.
7 Thomas Sprat, *The History of the Royal-Society of London, for the Improving of Natural Knowledge* (1667) p. 102.
8 The passage comes from his 'Resolution': Arthur Collins, *Proceedings, Precedents, and Arguments, on Claims and Controversies, concerning Baronies by Writ, and other Honours* (London 1734) pp. 176–7. A limited reprint of the relevant pages was published at Cambridge in 1928.
9 6 August 1763: Boswell *Life of Johnson*, ed. G. B. Hill, rev L. F. Powell, 6 vols. (Oxford 1934–50) vol. I, 471. Oliver Edwards (see below at note 20) reminded him that he had not allowed his college friends to use the word 'prodigious': *ibid.*, III, 303.
10 16 October 1769: *Life*, II, 82.
11 See his *Diaries, Prayers and Annals*, ed. E. L. McAdam Jr with D. and M. Hyde, *Works* I (New Haven 1958) pp. 46, 63, 71 etc.
12 *The Rambler*, ed. W. J. Bate and A. B. Straus, no. 110: *Works*, IV (New Haven 1969) p. 224.
13 20 April 1781: *Life*, V, 96–9.

14 *Life*, V, 5. For his general admiration see, e.g., *ibid.*, II, 125.

15 Johnson's quotation is to be found (*variatim*) in John Quincy's *Lexicon Physico-Medicum; or, a New Physical Dictionary* (1719) p. 183.

16 The latter point is a major theme in the second of his *Sermons*, ed. J. H. Hagstrum and J. Gray: *Works*, XIV (New Haven 1978) 17–27. A strict mental separation between his fears of being 'sent to Hell and being punished everlastingly' and his hopes of divine mercy can be traced in his conversation with Dr Adams of 12 June 1784: *Life*, IV, 299.

17 Among his examples of the verb 'to bottom' Johnson includes, from Atterbury, 'Every action is supposed to be bottomed upon some principle.'

18 *The Life and Opinions of Tristram Shandy, Gentleman*, 9 vols. (1760) vol. I, pp. 27–8. This is cited by Roy Porter, who also points out that James Hutton saw gravity as symbolically the power of 'death' in the universe, countered by heat as the principle of 'life': 'Against the Spleen' in *Lawrence Sterne: Riddles and Mysteries*, ed. Valerie Grosvenor Myer (1984) p. 88.

19 'Liberty in *Tristram Shandy*': *ibid.*, 127–8.

20 *Tristram Shandy*, VI, vii, 572. Dr Johnson, interestingly, could see only oddity; 'Nothing odd will do long – *Tristram Shandy* did not last': 20 March 1776, *Life*, II, 449.

21 17 April 1778: *Life*, III, 302–7.

22 'An Island in the Moon': Blake, *Writings*, ed. Geoffrey Keynes (1957) p. 54.

23 Lines 105–7: *Poetical Works*, ed. E. H. Coleridge, 2 vols. (Oxford 1912) vol. I, 113.

24 Letter to Sotheby of 1802, *Collected Letters*, II, 813–4.

25 *Aids to Reflection*, ed. John Beer, *The Collected Coleridge* 9, (Princeton, NJ and London 1993) p. 7 and n.

26 This was reproduced by Coleridge and Southey in their *Omniana* (1812) I, 241–2. An English translation can be found in Coleridge's *Notebooks*, ed. Kathleen Coburn, 5

volumes in progress (Princeton, NJ and London 1957–) vol. I, 929n.

27 'The Triumph of Life', lines 196–8: Shelley, *Poetical Works*, ed. T. Hutchinson (Oxford 1904) 560.

28 Notebook of 1908, quoted Quentin Bell, *Virginia Woolf: A Biography*, 2 vols. (1972) vol. I, 138.

29 Entry for 22 June 1940: *The Diary of Virginia Woolf*, ed. Anne Olivier Bell, 5 vols. (1977–84) vol. V, 298.

30 *The Journals and Papers of Gerard Manley Hopkins*, ed. Humphry House and Graham Storey (1959) p. 269. Geoffrey Hill cites part of this in the notes to his essay, 'Our Word is our Bond', to which I am indebted for two further references (33 and 34 below): see his *The Lords of Limit* (1984) pp. 151, 155 and nn.

31 Richard Chenevix Trench noted this in his *On the Study of Words* (1851) p. 63, quoted by J. Milroy in *The Language of Gerard Manley Hopkins* (1977) p. 82.

32 Some critics think that the action being described is that of the kestrel 'stooping', but opinion is divided: see *The Poetical Works of Gerard Manley Hopkins*, ed. Norman H. MacKenzie (Oxford 1990) p. 144 and note, pp. 379–80.

33 *The New Criticism* (Norfolk, Ct, 1949) p. 79.

34 *The Structure of Complex Words* (1951) p. 39.

35 Noel Stock, *Poet in Exile: Ezra Pound* (Manchester 1964) pp. 2–3. Stock also points out that the memory turns up as an image in Canto 97.

36 Chapter i: Jane Austen, *Northanger Abbey and Persuasion*, 4 vols. (1818) vol. III, 8.

37 Dickens, *Dealings with the Firm of Dombey and Son* (1848) ch. xvii, p. 166.

38 *Ibid.*, ch. xxii, p. 213.

39 When Mrs Thistlethwayte suggested they should burn their correspondence, he demurred, questioning the propriety of her use of 'great, deep, weighty words' such as 'love' and 'sadness' and asserting that human beings should retain the

means of calling themselves to account: 'Probably from the habits of my life I weigh my words more strictly than you do, and am more fully aware that it is often necessary to consider not only the sense in which we use them, but the sense which others will put upon them.' Letters of 23 and 27 October 1869: *Diaries* vol. VIII, ed. H. C. G. Matthew (Oxford 1982) pp. 569, 572.

40 T. H. Huxley, lecture of 1877 to the Working Men's Club and Institute, 'Technical Education', reprinted in *Science and Culture and other Essays* (1881) p. 82.

41 Steven Weinberg, *Dreams of a Final Theory* (1993) p. 102.

42 *Ibid.*, p. 196 and ch. vi *passim*.

43 *Ibid.*, pp. 208–9.

44 Daniel C. Dennett, *Consciousness Explained* (1991) p. 410 and chs. xiii–xiv.

45 A. S. Byatt, *Angels and Insects* (1992) p. 204.

46 *In Memoriam*, section x, lines 5–8.

47 *The Prelude* (1805) book viii, lines 703–6. All *Prelude* quotations are from Wordsworth, *The Prelude 1799, 1805, 1850* edited by J. Wordsworth, M. H. Abrams and S. Gill (New York 1979).

48 'There was a boy . . . ', *Poetical Works*, ed. E. de Selincourt and Helen Darbishire, 5 vols. (Oxford 1940–49) vol. II, 206; included later in *The Prelude* (1805) v, 389–413.

49 Letter of 10 December 1798: *Collected Letters*, I, 452–3.

50 'Calais, August 15, 1802', line 11: *Poetical Works*, III, 111.

51 *The Prelude* (1799) ii, 262–7.

52 Letter of 6 April 1799, *Collected Letters*, I, 479–50.

53 Quoted from *ibid.* When Wordsworth included the poem, untitled, in the 1800 *Lyrical Ballads* he changed 'mov'd' to 'rolled' and removed the final exclamation mark.

54 One may compare the still horse that he once contemplated in the moonlight, 'With all his functions silently sealed up . . . A living statue or a statued life': see the draft lines printed in *The Prelude*, (New York 1979) p. 498.

55 See *The White Doe of Rylstone*, dedication, lines 21–40: *Poetical Works*, III, 281–2.

56 Poetical Works, III, 16.

57 Shelley, *Poetical Works*, pp. 684–5.

58 Gillian Beer has drawn attention to this link in her edition of *The Waves* (Oxford 1992): see pp. xxxi, 44, 135, 170–1, 251.

59 Philip Larkin, *Collected Poems*, ed. A. Thwaite (1988) p. 106.

60 Marcel Proust, *Remembrance of Things Past*, tr. C. K. Scott-Moncrieff and T. Kilmartin, 3 vols. (1981) vol. II, 785.

61 See *The Prelude* (1805): e.g. i, 459, 479; ii, 135–8; iii, 358–63.

62 'Imagery and Movement: Notes in the Analysis of Movement', *Scrutiny* 1945, XIII, 126. Leavis finds the answer to his questioning in the development of the poem itself.

63 'Of Vicissitude of Things. LVIII': *Essayes*, pp. 172–6.

64 *Paradise Lost* vi, 393–4.

65 *Ibid.*, i, 3–6.

66 *Ibid.*, vii, 350–2.

67 *Ibid.*, vi, 4–8.

68 *Ibid.*, vi, 620–7 (italics mine).

69 *Ibid.*, 763–6.

70 Wordsworth, *Prose Works*, ed. W. J. B. Owen and J. W. Smyser, 3 vols. (Oxford 1974) vol. III, 34. Coleridge also praised the phrase as a triumph of the epic imagination, giving unity 'by throwing back into the distance': *Table Talk*, 23 June 1834, ed. Carl Woodring, *Collected Coleridge* 14, 2 vols. (1990) I, 490.

71 *Paradise Lost*, vi, 771–3.

For EU product safety concerns, contact us at Calle de José Abascal, 56–1°,
28003 Madrid, Spain or eugpsr@cambridge.org.

www.ingramcontent.com/pod-product-compliance
Ingram Content Group UK Ltd.
Pitfield, Milton Keynes, MK11 3LW, UK
UKHW012334130625
459647UK00009B/277